The Fault in Our Stars Classroom Questions

A SCENE BY SCENE TEACHING GUIDE

Amy Farrell

SCENE BY SCENE
ENNISKERRY, IRELAND

Copyright © 2015 by Amy Farrell.

All rights reserved. No part of this publication may be reproduced, distributed or transmitted in any form or by any means, including photocopying, recording, or other electronic or mechanical methods, without the prior written permission of the publisher, except in the case of brief quotations embodied in critical reviews and certain other noncommercial uses permitted by copyright law. For permission requests, write to the publisher, addressed "Attention: Permissions Coordinator," at the address below.

Scene by Scene
11 Millfield, Enniskerry
Wicklow, Ireland.
www.scenebysceneguides.com

The Fault in Our Stars Classroom Questions/Amy Farrell. —1st ed.
ISBN 978-1-910949-18-4

Contents

Chapter One	1
Chapter Two	3
Chapter Three	5
Chapter Four	6
Chapter Five	7
Chapter Six	9
Chapter Seven	10
Chapter Eight	11
Chapter Nine	12
Chapter Ten	13
Chapter Eleven	14
Chapter Twelve	15
Chapter Thirteen	17
Chapter Fourteen	19
Chapter Fifteen	20
Chapter Sixteen	21
Chapter Seventeen	22
Chapter Eighteen	23
Chapter Nineteen	24
Chapter Twenty	25
Chapter Twenty One	26

Chapter Twenty Two	27
Chapter Twenty Three	28
Chapter Twenty Four	29
Chapter Twenty Five	30

Chapter One

1. What happens at the Support Group?

2. What aspects of the story grab your interest in this opening chapter?
   What makes you want to find out more?

3. What is the only "redeeming facet" of Support Group? What makes the speaker say this?

4. Does Hazel have a good relationship with her mother, from what we have read so far?

5. Why does Hazel go to Support Group in the end? How does this make you feel, as you read it?

6. What is your reaction to learning of Hazel's oxygen tank?

7. How do you react to the teenagers' personal stories at Support Group?

8. What do we learn about Augustus in this chapter?

9. "…battles won amid wars sure to be lost…" Describe the atmosphere at Support Group. Describe Hazel's outlook.

10. Do you feel sorry for Hazel? Explain your reasons fully.

11. Is there humour in this chapter?
How does it add to the story?

12. How does Hazel react to Augustus' cigarette?

13. Do you want to read more as the chapter ends?
What makes you say this?

14. Would you have gone with Augustus? Explain your answer.

15. What do you learn about the speaker in chapter one?

16. What is the mood in this chapter? What makes you say this?

Chapter Two

1. What makes Augustus such a bad driver?

2. Why is Hazel reluctant to admit she's not in school? How does this affect the mood of the story?

3. Describe Hazel's "miracle".

4. "I finally ended up in the ICU with pneumonia." What makes this an emotional scene?

5. How does Hazel's description of her illness make you feel?

6. Describe Gus' home.

7. Describe Gus' relationship with his parents.

8. What gives Gus' parents comfort when struggling with his illness?

9. Are Gus' parents nice to Hazel?

10. Is there anything significant in Gus' story about giving up basketball?

11. Is there chemistry between Hazel and Gus? Does this add to the story?

12. Is Hazel keen on the 'Encouragements' in Gus' house? Does this reveal anything about her character?

13. Do Hazel and Gus sound like 'real' teenagers? How does this affect the story?

14. Gus is very keen to see Hazel again. She tells him, "You don't want to seem overeager." Do you think she is put off by his interest in her?

Chapter Three

1. Did Hazel like Gus' book?

2. What is Kaitlyn, Hazel's friend, like?

3. "…I knew it would surprise and amaze her that anyone as dishevelled and awkward and stunted as me could even briefly win the affections of a boy."
   How does Hazel view herself? Is she a typical teenager in this, or does her illness play a role here?

4. Does Hazel enjoy shopping with Kaitlyn?

5. Has Hazel's illness affected her relationships with friends and family? Explain, using examples to support your view.

6. "Anyway, I really did like being alone."
   Do you believe Hazel here?

7. What interests you about this story so far?

8. Is Hazel a good choice of narrator? Explain your view.

9. What additional information about Hazel's illness did you learn in this chapter?

10. How does this information add to the mood of the book?

Chapter Four

1. What is Hazel's favourite book about?
   Why does she like it so much?

2. Why has Hazel written so many letters to Peter Van Houten?

3. "Flirting was new to me, but I liked it." Describe Hazel's relationship with Augustus, at this point.

4. Why is Isaac so upset when Hazel goes over to Gus' house? Is this a realistic reaction, do you think?

5. Does Augustus take Isaac's problem seriously? Explain your view.

6. What is significant about Augustus' response to reading *An Imperial Affliction*?

Chapter Five

1. How does the author remind us of Hazel's illness, without mentioning cancer itself? How do these reminders add to the story's atmosphere?

2. Why has Augustus taken so long to phone Hazel? Does this tell you anything about his personality?

3. What is your reaction to Peter Van Houten's letter to Augustus?

4. If you were Peter Van Houten, would you be moved by Hazel's email?

5. Hazel finds out that Augustus' last girlfriend died from cancer. How would you feel about this, in Hazel's position?

6. Augustus' text tells Hazel that Isaac is cancer-free, but blind. How would you feel, if you were Isaac?

7. Is Hazel too understanding when her mother tells her she can't go to Amsterdam? Would you be so understanding?

8. "Augustus Waters was sitting on the front step as we pulled into the driveway." In your view, is Augustus romantic, or simply trying too hard? Explain your stance.

9. "…Hazel is still sick, Augustus, and will be for the rest of her life…" Does Hazel get to be a 'normal' teenager, in your opinion, or has her illness robbed her of this?

10. "I worried the cancer had spread from my lungs."
Why is Hazel worrying about this? Do you understand her concern?

11. "….not wanting to let myself imagine that all this would lead to Amsterdam…" Has knowing Augustus improved Hazel's life, in your opinion? Explain your view.

12. Describe the mood as this chapter ends.
How do you feel about the teenagers' trip to Amsterdam becoming a reality?

Chapter Six

1. "Augustus was amazing, but he'd overdone everything at the picnic…" Is Hazel being hard on Augustus here?

2. "…The realized touch…it was all wrong." What is your response to Hazel's reluctance to kiss Augustus?

3. "I'm a grenade and at some point I'm going to blow up and I would like to minimize the casualties, okay?"
What is your response to Hazel's outburst here?

4. Based on what you read in this chapter, what do you think of Hazel's parents and the relationship she has with them?

5. How do Hazel's worsening headaches contribute to the mood of the story?

Chapter Seven

1. What caused Hazel's headache?

2. "It wore me out." Is it easy to accept Hazel's poor health?

3. What impression of Peter Van Houten are you forming as the tale unfolds?

Chapter Eight

1. How does the Cancer Team Meeting affect the mood of the story?

2. What is the prognosis for Hazel, as you understand it?

3. "They might be glad to have me around, but I was the alpha and the omega of my parents' suffering."
What is your response to this thought of Hazel's?

4. Is Green giving us a realistic insight into the life of a cancer patient, in your view?

5. How is Hazel's relationship with Augustus developing? Do you like this aspect of the story?

6. "As he read, I fell in love the way you fall asleep: slowly, and then all at once." Comment on this sentence.

7. Do you feel hopeful as the chapter ends? Explain your standpoint.

Chapter Nine

1. Do you think Hazel benefits from attending Support Group?

2. Does Hazel have fun with Isaac?

3. Is Hazel an insightful person? Explain your answer.

Chapter Ten

1. What is the mood like as the chapter begins?

2. Based on all you have read so far, do you think Hazel has a good understanding of what life is like for her parents?

3. What's going on as Hazel and her mother arrive at Gus' house?

4. "The pain was always there…."
   Is Hazel brave, in your opinion?

5. "I could feel everybody watching us, wondering what was wrong with us…." How would you feel in Hazel's position?

6. Death is mentioned a lot in this section. Is there a morbid atmosphere in this chapter?

7. Describe the moment when Augustus tells Hazel he loves her. Is this a romantic moment, in your estimation?

8. "I couldn't say anything back." Describe the action and the atmosphere as this chapter ends.

Chapter Eleven

1. Describe Amsterdam as the characters arrive.

2. How does the setting of Amsterdam contribute to the mood in this chapter?

3. "The beautiful couple is beautiful."
   How do you feel as you read about the date at Oranjee? Does anything about it strike you as particularly sad, romantic or moving?

4. "…the trip itself was a cancer perk."
   Does Hazel's illness pervade every aspect of her life?

5. What do Hazel and Augustus argue about after dessert? Can you see her point of view?

6. "I could be worse." Would Augustus make a good boyfriend for Hazel, in your view?

7. Does Augustus telling Hazel about Caroline Mathers develop their relationship? Explain your answer.

8. What was Augustus' relationship with Caroline like?

9. How does Gus' story about Caroline add to the mood of the chapter?

Chapter Twelve

1. Describe Peter Van Houten. Is he a likeable character?

2. "…you say you don't want pity, but your very existence depends upon it." What is your reaction to Van Houten's hurtful remarks in this chapter?

3. Are you disappointed by how the meeting with Van Houten went, or were you expecting something like this?

4. *An Imperial Affliction* is a very special book for Hazel and Gus. Do you have a favourite novel? What do you like about it?

5. Do you feel sorry for Lidewij here?

6. Why does the Anne Frank house pose a challenge for Hazel?

7. "And then we were kissing." Why, do you think, does Hazel kiss Augustus now?

8. What makes Augustus pause before taking Hazel to his room?

9. How would you describe the intimate scene between Hazel and Augustus? How does it contribute to the storyline?

Chapter Thirteen

1. "You have a choice in this world, I believe, about how to tell sad stories, and we made the funny choice…"
   Does this idea relate to this novel itself? Explain your view.

2. Why does Hazel think there's something wrong as she walks back to the hotel with Augustus?

3. "I always thought he could love me because he'd once been sick. Only now did it occur to me that maybe he still was."
   What is your reaction to Hazel's realisation that Augustus may be ill again?

4. What did Augustus' PET scan reveal?
   What is your response to this?

5. "I couldn't unlove Augustus Waters. And I didn't want to."
   What is John Green telling us about love here, through Hazel's love for Augustus?

6. "I'm okay. I'll find a way to hang around and annoy you for a long time."
   What is your response to Augustus' determination to live?

7. "He was too smart for the kinds of solace I could offer." What makes it difficult for Hazel to offer Gus real comfort here?

8. Why doesn't Hazel break down when she hears Gus' news?

9. Describe the mood as the chapter ends.

10. Has anything changed in how you view and feel about Gus? Explain.

Chapter Fourteen

1. "So I read *An Imperial Affliction* while you guys were gone."
   Does Hazel have a good relationship with her father?

2. How do you feel as you read about Gus joking with Isaac about his illness?

3. Why did Gus ask Hazel if she had four dollars?

4. Were they right to egg Monica's car, in your view?

5. "I never took another picture of him."
   Are things happening very fast? Are you prepared for Gus' decline?

Chapter Fifteen

1. Are Hazel and Gus making the most of their time together? Do you find this sad or uplifting?

2. "You know we love you, Hazel, but right now we just need to be a family."
   What is your reaction to Gus' mother preventing Hazel from seeing him in the hospital?

3. How do you feel as this chapter ends?

4. Do you want to read on? Explain.

Chapter Sixteen

1. How has his illness changed Gus? How does this make you feel?

2. Are you saddened by a "typical day with late-stage Gus"?

3. Gus says, "It is a good life, Hazel Grace". Are you surprised by his contentment here?

4. What is life like for Gus' parents?

Chapter Seventeen

1. "…I was hoping he didn't remember that I'd found the boy I love deranged in a wide pool of his own piss."
   Comment on this line.

2. What is significant about Hazel calling Augustus, 'Gus' now?

3. "I just want to be enough for you, but I never can be."
   Can you appreciate each character's perspective here? Who is right and who is wrong?

4. What is happening to Hazel and Augustus' relationship?

Chapter Eighteen

1. Why does Augustus ring Hazel in the middle of the night?

2. What was her immediate reaction to the call?
   How does this affect the mood of the story?

3. What condition is Gus in when Hazel reaches him?

4. Why did he go to the gas station?
   Can you appreciate why he did this?

5. "…just let me fucking die." What is your response to Augustus' upset?

6. What does the author mean by "the conventions of the genre"? Why has he sought to break these conventions?

7. Comment on the image the chapter ends on, as the teenagers wait for the ambulance to find them.

Chapter Nineteen

1. Why does Augustus feel he's lost his dignity?
   Is there truth in what he says?

2. What do you think of Augustus' family and how they behave towards him?

3. What is your response to Hazel and Augustus' gallows humour in this chapter?

4. How do you feel at this point in the story?

Chapter Twenty

1. What does Hazel have a disagreement with her parents about? Is she unfair here?

2. Do you find Augustus' desire for a prefuneral morbid or natural? Explain.

3. What is your reaction to Isaac's eulogy?

4. What is your reaction to Hazel's eulogy?

5. What is the mood like as the chapter ends?

6. How does Augustus' humour add to this mood?

Chapter Twenty One

1. According to Hazel, what do her parents feel when they learn of Augustus' death? Do you think she's right in this instance?

2. "The only person I really wanted to talk to about Augustus Waters's death was Augustus Waters." Explain this line. How is Hazel feeling?

3. How well is Hazel coping with Augustus' death?

4. What's interesting about the condolences on Augustus' "wall page"?

5. What do you make of Hazel's post on his page? Does it tell you anything about her?

6. How do Hazel's parents help her with her grief?

Chapter Twenty Two

1. How does reading about Gus' funeral make you feel?

2. How does the minister annoy Hazel?

3. What does Isaac's speech at the funeral tell you about Gus' character?

4. "…I, like everyone in that room, would go on accumulating loves and losses while he would not."
   Is this a sad thought, in your view?

5. "It looked like any other funeral." Why is Hazel so against Augustus' funeral? Do you sympathise with her at all?

6. What is your reaction to Peter Van Houten turning up at Gus' funeral?

7. What is your reaction to the way Hazel treats him?

8. "…I had already seen everything pure and good in the world…" How is Hazel feeling?

9. "My old man. He always knew just what to say."
   How does Hazel's dad help make her feel better?

Chapter Twenty Three

1. What is your reaction to Van Houten turning up in Hazel's car?

2. Do you pity Van Houten at all?

3. What does Hazel realise about the drunk author? Does this change your view of him? Does it change Hazel's?

4. Do you think Gus' parents are coping with their grief?

5. "I just shook my head no…" Were you expecting Hazel to find something? How does this contribute to the mood?

Chapter Twenty Four

1. Are you surprised when Hazel tells Patrick she wishes she "would just die"?

2. What reasons does Hazel have for living?

3. "I won't stop being your mom."
   What is your response to the emotion in this chapter?

4. Why does her mother taking some online classes make Hazel happy?

5. What is your response to Hazel's honest conversation with her parents? Does anything surprise you? How does it make you feel?

Chapter Twenty Five

1. Is Kaitlyn a good friend?

2. "But thinking about Lidewij and her boyfriend, I felt robbed." What makes Hazel feel this way?

3. "All I know of heaven and all I know of death is in this park…" What do Hazel's thoughts as she picnics with her parents, reveal about her?

4. What is your response to Augustus' letter to Van Houten?

5. Read the last paragraph of Augustus' letter again. Bearing in mind that it was written when he was approaching his death, what is the tone of the letter?

6. How do you feel, as you finish reading this novel?

7. What is the point of the 'Author's Note' at the end?

8. As readers, were we grieving for Augustus from the moment we learned about his PET scan results?

9. Does the author try to teach us anything in this novel? What is his message for us?

10. Is there humour in this story? Explain.

11. What was Van Houten's role in the story? Why was this character significant?

12. Did you enjoy this story? Explain your view.

WWW.SCENEBYSCENEGUIDES.COM

Visit www.scenebysceneguides.com to see our full catalogue of Classroom Questions and Workbooks.

Hamlet Scene by Scene Classroom Questions

Romeo and Juliet Scene by Scene Classroom Questions

King Lear Scene by Scene Classroom Questions

Macbeth Scene by Scene Classroom Questions

A Doll's House Classroom Questions

Animal Farm Classroom Questions

Foster Classroom Questions

Good Night, Mr. Tom Classroom Questions

WWW.SCENEBYSCENEGUIDES.COM

Subscribe to our newsletter at www.scenebysceneguides.com/newsletter to keep up to date with all the latest title releases.

Martyn Pig Classroom Questions

Of Mice and Men Classroom Questions

Pride and Prejudice Classroom Questions

Private Peaceful Classroom Questions

The Fault in Our Stars Classroom Questions

The Old Man and the Sea Classroom Questions

The Outsiders Classroom Questions

To Kill a Mockingbird Classroom Questions

The Spinning Heart Classroom Questions

www.ingramcontent.com/pod-product-compliance
Lightning Source LLC
Chambersburg PA
CBHW071507080526
44587CB00016B/2717